Fishing

Rebecca Hunter

Photography by Chris Fairclough

First published in 2009 by
Franklin Watts
338 Euston Road
London NW1 3BH

Franklin Watts Australia
Level 17/207 Kent Street
Sydney NSW 2000

A CIP catalogue record for this book is available from the British Library.

Planning and production by Discovery Books Limited
Editor: Rebecca Hunter
Designer: Ian Winton
Illustrator: Stefan Chabluk
Photography: Chris Fairclough
Additional photography: Peter Steele Mortimer: Cover, p.6, p.7 top, p.23
bottom, p.24 top, p.25, p.26 top; Istockphoto.com: p. 8 top (Timur Kulgarin); p. 8
bottom (Svetlana Shapiro) p. 9 (Evgeny Kan); p. 16 top (Judy Ledbetter);
p. 22 bottom (Paul Tessier); p. 23 top (Yevgen Timashov); p. 24 bottom
(Jon Helgason); p. 27 top; p. 27 bottom (Abel Leáo).

Consultant: Peter Steele Mortimer, a lifelong fisherman!

The author, packager and publisher would like to thank the following people for
their participation in this book: George, Ben and Jess Steele Mortimer, Harry
and Brian Swaithe, Delbury Hall Trout Fishery and Ludlow Tackle, Ludlow.

Printed in China

Franklin Watts is a division of Hachette Children's Books,
an Hachette UK company.
www.hachette.co.uk

Contents

Introduction to fishing

Fishing, or angling, is probably the oldest sport in the world. In Britain today, it is also the most popular. There are three main types of fishing: sea fishing, **game fishing** and **coarse fishing**. This book is mainly about coarse fishing.

Anyone can learn to fish. All you need is a fishing rod and a suitable place to fish. Coarse fishing is done on lakes and ponds, or on waterways such as rivers and canals.

Safety facts
- Learn how to swim.
- Always fish with an adult nearby.
- Do not enter the water to get things you have dropped.

You can fish almost all year, except for a few weeks in spring when the fish are **breeding**. This is called the closed season.

Equipment

Fishing equipment is called tackle. The main items are a rod and **reel** and a net for landing the fish.

No particular clothing is needed for coarse fishing. You should dress according to the weather. If it is sunny, shorts, a T-shirt and a hat will be fine. If rain is likely bring waterproofs and an umbrella. A fishing vest can be useful as it has many pockets to hold equipment.

Other important things to remember are sunscreen, sunglasses, some food and drink and a note book and camera to record your catch.

Rod

Fishing vest

Reel

Fish and where to find them

Before you set out on your fishing trip,
you will need to know what fish you are most likely to catch,
where to find them and what equipment you will need.

Types of fish

The carp (above) is one of the biggest fish you are likely to catch. It used to be found in still waters such as lakes and ponds, but now is often found in rivers and canals too. Carp grow to over 30kg, so if you plan to catch a big one you will need a special carp rod.

Bream (below) are a very common fish in inland waters. They have a very wide body. Young fish are silver coloured but older ones often look golden. They feed on the bottom of ponds and lakes so you will need to weight your **bait** to catch a bream.

The pike (below) is one of the most exciting freshwater fish to catch. It is a fierce **predator**, **preying** on all types of fish, including smaller pike.

Pike live in the open water of rivers, lakes and ponds. Pike usually weigh about 10kg, although the largest ever caught was over 25kg. You will need a strong line and a live bait or **lure** to catch a pike.

Trout are normally fished for in fast-flowing upland rivers with a **fly** (see page 24) but visiting a private trout pond is often a good way for a beginner to start. Using bait such as grubs or maggots and a **float**, you are likely to be successful, as these ponds are stocked daily.

Rods, reels and lines

Most rods are made of **carbon fibre** or **fibreglass**. They are strong and flexible and usually come in two or three sections which you fit together. The handle is covered with cork or foam so it is comfortable to hold. All rods have a series of rings along them through which the line passes. The thinnest part of the rod at the top end is called the tip.

Handle

Rings

Tip

The sections are quite easy to fit together. The solid end of the lower section fits into the hollow end of the upper section. You must make sure the rings on the rod all line up.

Reels

The most popular type of reel and the easiest for a beginner to use, is the fixed-spool reel. All fixed-spool reels have a metal lever called the **bale arm**. This keeps the line from

Foot

Bale arm

Spool

Reel handle

slipping off the reel. It can also be opened up to allow the line to run freely during **casting**. The reel handle is used to wind in the line. It can be attached on either the right or left side, depending on whether you are right- or left-handed.

Lines

Fishing line is made of nylon and is transparent – so the fish can't see it!

It comes in different strengths depending on what type of fish you hope to catch and how heavy they might be. For most coarse fishing, a 3lb (1.5kg) line is fine. For **leger fishing** you will need a stronger, 8lb (3.2kg) line.

11

The tackle box

As well as a rod, reel and line, you need a net to land your fish and a tackle box to keep the rest of your equipment in. Tackle boxes are made of plastic and come in many sizes.

Swivels

Swivels can be used to attach the main line to the hook length. They spin so the line can turn without becoming twisted. ——————

Scissors ——————

For cutting lines.

Floats ——————

Floats come in many different shapes and sizes. They are brightly coloured so you can see them easily.

Lures ——————

Lures are made to look like small fish that other fish will want to eat. They have one or more **treble hooks** attached to them.

Landing net
This is for landing your catch.

Tackle box

Hooks

Hooks should be barbless (without a **barb**) so that they are easy to remove from the fish's mouth without damaging the fish.

Float rings

Float rings are used to attach the float to the line (see page 18).

Weighing scales

Weighing scales to weigh your catch.

Split shot

Split shot is attached to the line in float fishing to weigh the line down and hold the bait at the right level (see page 18).

Lines

Bait

Bait is for attracting the fish (see page 16).

Weights

Weights are used in leger fishing to keep the hook near the bottom of the river or lake.

Knots

One of the first things you need to learn in fishing is how to tie knots. Without a proper knot on your line, your hook will come loose and your fish will be lost.

Hook lengths

A hook length is a short piece of line that has a hook on one end and is attached to the main line at the other. The hook is attached with a half-blood knot. At the other end of the hook length, a simple loop knot connects it to the main line with a loop-to-loop knot.

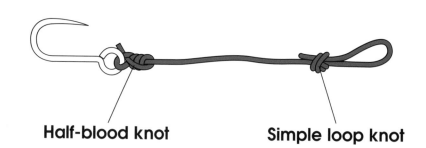

Half-blood knot   **Simple loop knot**

Half-blood knot

The half-blood knot is what you use to attach a line to a hook.

1. Thread about 7cm of line through the eye of the hook and double it back on itself.

2. Turn the hook around, so the line twists about 4 or 5 times.

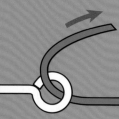

3. Keep the twist tight and thread the loose end through the loop nearest the hook.

4. Pull the end tight then trim off the end.

Simple loop knot

The simple loop knot is what you make on the end of the main line and on the other end of the hook length.

1. Fold about 10cm of line back on itself.

2. Make the double line into a loose ring, and push the folded end through it.

3. Pull the two ends of the line apart to tighten the knot. Cut the spare bit of line off close to the knot.

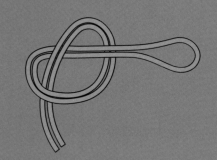

Loop-to-loop knot

This is the knot you need to join the hook length to the main line.

1. Place the hook length loop over the main line loop.

2. Thread the hook back through the main line loop from below.

3. Pull the two lines apart and the knot will tighten.

Hook length

Main line

Floats and bait

Using a float is a way of holding the hook at the right level in the water and showing you when a fish has bitten. (Your float wobbles or disappears.) There are many different sizes and shapes of float for using in different types of water.

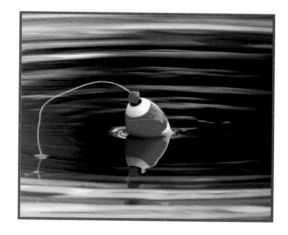

Stick floats and bob floats are the most useful kinds of floats. The line is attached to both ends of the float at a length along the line that is suitable for the depth of the water.

Bait

Fish are attracted to the hook by bait. Bait can be any type of food that fish want to eat. Different fish like different baits so you need to experiment and try out a few different things.

Bread, pasta, cheese, sweetcorn and jellybeans (left) can all be used as bait.

Many fish prefer living bait such as worms (right) or maggots (below). You can dig up worms yourself from the garden, and maggots and grubs can be bought from a tackle store.

Groundbait

Groundbait is made of broken up bread and biscuits and can be thrown into the area where you are fishing to attract fish. Don't use too much or the fish won't be hungry any more.

Live bait and lures

Some fish prefer to eat real fish. You can either use live bait, which consists of small, live fish such as minnows, or you could use a lure. Lures are made from wood, plastic or metal, and are made to look like small fish. Fishing using a lure is called spinning.

Assembling the rod

Attaching the reel

The reel attaches to the handle of the rod by placing the foot of the reel between the reel fittings (right). The spool should face the tip of the rod and the rings on the rod should face down.

Assemble the rod then thread the line through each of the rings (below).

Slide two float rings onto the end of the line about 1 metre from the end. Attach the float to the line with the float rings. The bright end of the float should point towards the rod. Tie a loop knot in the end of the line.

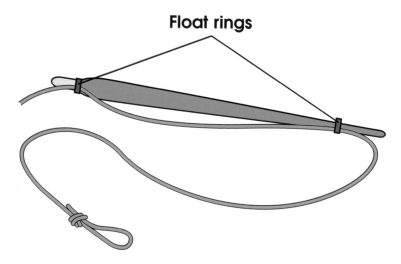

Float rings

Squeeze three or four split shot onto the line (right) below the float.

Baiting a hook

Now attach your hook length to the loop at the end of the line using a loop-to-loop knot. If you are using live worms as bait, make sure the hook goes right through the worm so that the hook goes right into the fish's mouth. Your rod is now ready for fishing!

Casting

Casting is what you do to get your hook in the water. There are two ways you can cast depending on where in the water you want to fish.

Underarm casting

To catch fish that swim near the edge of the water you can cast using the underarm method.

1. Start by holding the rod in one hand with the hook and bait near the reel. Press the line coming off the reel against the rod handle with your finger. Open the bale arm by pulling it over the spool.

Overhead casting

Overhead casting lets you get the bait further away from the bank.

1. Hold the rod with both hands, so that its tip is above your head and behind you.

2. Hold the line against the rod and open the bale arm – as before in underarm casting.

2. Tip the rod forward slightly, swing the hook over the water, and let go of the line you are holding.

3. When the bait hits the water, turn the reel handle so that the bale arm flips over and the line tightens.

4. Underarm casting is useful when there are trees and bushes nearby, as it doesn't need much space.

3. Jerk the rod forward towards the water and when your top arm is straight, take your finger off the line.

4. When the bait hits the water, turn the reel and tighten the line.

Playing and landing

When you see your float move and feel a tug on your line, you know a fish has bitten. Although this is a thrilling moment, you haven't caught the fish until it is out of the water and on the bank!

Playing

First you need to 'play' your fish. This means keeping it on the line and tiring it out. As the fish swims away from you, let more line out. If it swims nearer to you and the line slackens, lift the rod up or reel

some line in, to stop the fish wriggling off the hook.

Riverside rules
- Check before casting that nobody is within striking distance.
- Don't discard old line, weights or broken hooks.
- Keep quiet on the riverbank.
- Don't leave litter.

Landing

Landing a fish means getting it out of water. A small fish may be easy to land, but a larger one needs a net and preferably a friend to help. Reel the fish in close to the water's

edge. Don't try to lift it out of the water. Get your friend to move the net under the fish. Lift the net out of the water and remove the hook from the fish's mouth.

Weighing and recording

Now you can weigh your fish on the weighing scales. Take a photo of you and your catch too!

Record the weight, length and type of fish in a notebook. Record when and where you caught the fish, and what the weather and water conditions were like. This way you can build up knowledge of how to be more successful at fishing. After weighing it, release the fish back into the water.

Fly fishing and surf fishing

When you have mastered the art of coarse fishing, you may wish to try another kind. Both fly fishing and surf fishing offer new challenges and the chance to catch fish that you can take home, cook and eat!

Fly fishing is a method of catching fish, usually trout or salmon, in fast-flowing upland rivers. Fly fishermen often wear **waders** (above) so they can walk up and down in the river.

Flies

The fly fisherman uses a fly instead of bait or lures. Flies are made of brightly coloured feathers and look like real, living

insects. The fly is cast on the surface of the water and is then reeled in slowly. Fly fishing in fast water can be dangerous. You will need to be taught by an experienced fisherman.

Surf fishing

Surf fishing involves fishing from the shoreline. You will need a very long fishing rod and suitable spinning reel. You also need a large float and a weight. At the end of your line could be a lure or spinner, or more likely some live bait, such as lugworms, sand-eels or other small fish.

Surfcasting or beachcasting is the method of casting the line into the sea a long distance from the beach. The line is left in the water until a fish bites. A surf fisherman needs to be patient and a rod holder and chair are other useful pieces of equipment!

Saltwater fish you are likely to catch include mullet, wrasse, cod, mackerel and sea bass.

Clubs and competitions

The best way to start fishing is to join an angling club. A club will tell you where you can fish and may even have rights to certain stretches of river.

Rod Fishing Licence
Salmon and Freshwater Fisheries Act 1975

This licence authorises the angler described here, and no other, to fish with single rod and line for non migratory trout (brown and rainbow) and char, or with up to two rods and line (where byelaws and rules permit) for freshwater fish and eels during the period covered by this licence in all waters within the area of the Environment Agency, subject to the close seasons, the Environment Agency fisheries byelaws and the permission of the fishery owners.

Full and concessionary rod licences are valid from the date of purchase or 1st April 2008 if purchased before this date. It is not permitted for 1 and 8 day rod licences to be valid prior to the time and date of issue.

Full & concessionary rod licences expire on 31st March 2009.

If you have answered yes to the marketing question then we may pass your name and address to other companies or organisations who can provide you with further information about fishing or fishing related products and services e.g. angling clubs, fishing magazines, tackle retailers etc. We may also use your name and postal address to send you similar information on behalf of other companies and organisations.

| Licence Category | Trout and Coarse |
| Licence Type | Junior Concession |

Forename

Surname

Home Address

Postcode

Date Of Birth   07/05/19

Gender   Male

Marketing Info Requested   No

Issue Date&Time 18/08/200   11:40

DUTY PAID   £5.00

Licence Number   TJ2638

9826 9361 0400 2638 0546

Licences and permits

All anglers, over 12 years of age, who are fishing for freshwater fish in England, Wales and Northern Ireland must have a rod licence. (Check the licence requirements for a river in Scotland or Australia before you fish.)

You may also need a fishing permit to fish on water that belongs to a club or fishery. A club will tell you what size and number of fish you can keep. In most clubs all fish have to be returned to water.

Competitions

A fishing competition is called a match and many clubs and fisheries run matches for junior anglers during the holidays.

The National Junior Angling Association (NJAA) hosts three major competitions every year that are open to any junior fishing teams.

Glossary

bait anything that is put on a hook to catch fish

bale arm a lever on a fishing reel that stops the line from slipping off

barb a small part that sticks out at the end of some fish hooks so they stick more firmly in a fish's mouth

breeding laying eggs or reproducing

carbon fibre a strong, light material made of fibres of carbon

casting a method of throwing your hook into the water

coarse fishing fishing for freshwater fish that do not belong to the salmon family

fibreglass a strong, light material made of thin fibres of glass

float a plastic device on a fishing line that keeps the hook at the right depth

fly a hook that is disguised with feathers or fur to look like a real insect: for fly fishing

game fishing fishing for sport – usually for salmon or trout

leger fishing using weights to help you catch fish near the bottom of the water

lure things that are made to look like small fish to attract bigger fish

predator an animal that eats other animals

preying eating other animals

reel the wheel at the end of the fishing rod that winds in the line

treble hooks three hooks joined together

waders an outfit of waterproof boots and trousers that lets you wade in rivers without getting wet

Further reading

Fishing: Get Outdoors, Nick Ross, Wayland, 2008

Go Fishing and Catch Fish: How To…, Gareth Purnell, Franklin Watts, 2007

The Little Book of Fishing Tips, Michael Devenish, Absolute Press, 2007

Starting Fishing: Usborne First Skills, Lesley Sims and H. Edon, Usborne Publishing Ltd, 2004

Begin Fishing the Right Way, Ian Ball Elliot, Right Way Books, 1999

Further information

National Federation of Anglers
National Water Sports Centre
Adbolton Lane
Holme Pierrepont
Nottingham
NG12 2LU
Email: office@nfadirect.com
Website: www.nfadirect.com

Recfish Australia
PO Box 187
Grange
Qld 4051
Email: admin@recfish.com.au
Website: www.recfish.com.au

Index